Oprah Winfrey: A Biography

Billionaire Media Mogul and Philanthropist

"Where there is no struggle, there is no strength." As a woman entering a world dominated by men, Oprah Winfrey's life is nothing short of a living testament to her words. Oprah Winfrey, daughter of a single mother, would have been given every excuse to live the life her mother had lived, a life of poverty and submission. However, Oprah grew to recognize the fallacy of being put into a lifestyle rather than choosing one. Oprah did not choose a lifestyle of wealth and fame, but was rather placed on the pedestal she now enjoys simply due to her courage to take a stand against the oppressive conditions women faced, and continue to face. Though a victim of unspeakable hatred and injustice at a young age, Oprah chose to rise above the sorrow and exchange it for courage. As Oprah once said, "The biggest adventure you can take is to live the life of your dreams." Oprah chose the life of change, the life of compassion, and most of all, the life of courage. Many have asserted that Oprah is the most influential person of the 21st century, and her Midas touch of success would vouch for that.

Through the life of Oprah Winfrey, anyone can be inspired to live a life founded on the courage to change.

Oprah Gail Winfrey was born on January 29, 1954 to un-married Vernon Winfrey and Vernita Lee in rural Koscuisko, Mississippi. Though Oprah's birth certificate reads Orpah Winfrey, as in the Orpah described in the Bible, people commonly mispronounced her name and both Oprah and her parents accepted the mispronunciation as her new name. Oprah describes her parents' relationship as "A summertime fling under an Oak tree" and they did not stay in a relationship long after her birth. Soon, the young girl was living with only her mother. Oprah's mother was a housemaid who regularly had to work long hours to procure enough of an income to support both herself and her daughter. Oprah's father was a coal miner who would later delve into the trade of barbering before serving as a city councilman. At the time of Oprah's birth, her father was serving in the Armed Forces. After the couple split up, Oprah's mother took Oprah and returned to the house of Vernita's mother, where the two entered the life of poverty Oprah's mother had so long endured. Hattie Mae Lee, Oprah's grandmother, was in such dire poverty that Oprah was forced to wear potato sacks as dresses. This hardship was only made worse by the continual mocking of the local children. Oprah's grandmother, though poor as she was, knew the value of handwork and refused to let Oprah's education suffer in her current conditions. Using every chance possible to educate Oprah, Oprah's grandmother taught Oprah to read before she was three and taught her numerous Bible verses. At the local church Oprah attended with her grandmother, Oprah garnered the nickname "The Preacher" as a result of her ability to recite Biblical passages so accurately. Oprah's grandmother also taught Oprah obedience, regularly striking Oprah with a wooden stick if she disobeyed in any fashion. At an early age, Oprah was being taught the value of obedience while also being taught that independence and education were secondary only to hard work in the pursuit of excellence in the world.

While living on the farm with only herself to entertain her, Oprah would use the farm animals as an audience and act out plays she made up in front of them. Oprah demonstrated intense independence at a young age, even skipping kindergarten entirely by means of a note she wrote saying she was supposed to be in first grade. This premature promotion did not harm the education of Oprah, and she was soon enrolled in third grade after skipping second grade entirely. After turning six years old, Oprah moved with her mother and two half brothers to a neighborhood in Milwaukee, Wisconsin. The neighborhood was extremely dangerous with shootings and drug-related activities happening almost nightly.

Oprah's grandmother had fallen gravely ill and died soon after Oprah left. In Milwaukee, Oprah was away from the encouragement and support of her grandmother, and her mother Vernita was hardly the mentor her mother had been. Oprah was left mostly to care for herself as her mother continued to work long hours to provide for her small family. Even as just a six year old, Oprah was often tasked with taking care of her infant sister as well. During these years of hard times, Oprah was known for her intelligence and independence. At her mother's church, Oprah become known as "The Little Speaker" in regards to her knack for saying the right thing at the right time. When Oprah turned eight, her mother decided she could no longer care for Oprah along with her other siblings, so Oprah was sent to live with her father in Nashville, Tennessee. Prior to leaving, Oprah stole an undisclosed amount of money from her mother, something she would regret for the entirety of her stay with her father and stepmother. Oprah's father and stepmother were more than happy to house the young girl because Oprah's stepmother, Zelma, was unable to have children. Oprah's mother would give birth to another daughter while Oprah was in Nashville, but this daughter would be placed for adoption due to the financial strain Oprah's mother was struggling with. In Nashville, Oprah gained more independence and soon found she had a natural ability for public speaking. After giving a number of speeches, Oprah determined she would like to continue speaking but was unsure of the feasibility in creating a career out of such a talent. Oprah's uncertainties were dispelled when she was awarded $500 for a speech she gave. After earning this money, Oprah became certain that a career was possible, and more than that, Oprah wanted to "be paid to talk." Shortly after this revelation, Oprah's mother decided she could once again handle the responsibility of mothering all of her children, so Oprah was sent back to live with her mother. Shortly after Oprah returned home, her mother gave birth to yet another child, Oprah's half-brother Jeffrey. Though Oprah was thankful to be back with her mother, Oprah would begin to experience many of the hardships facing young women around our world today. However, accompanying these days of hurt would be days of strength and victory. These days would lay the foundation for the life Oprah would live someday as an influential leader and courageous individual.

At the young age of nine, Oprah first experienced sexual abuse, the first of many tragic encounters. Oprah's 19 year-old cousin raped her while she was babysitting her siblings. After the encounter took place, Oprah's cousin took her to a local ice cream shop, bought her an ice cream cone, and instructed Oprah to never tell anyone about the abuse. Oprah complied for the time being, but sadly, this moment would not be the last. Many episodes like the previous would happen over the next few years, breaking the heart of Oprah, but not her will. Though Oprah would be raped and sexually abused by her uncle, cousin, and a family friend, Oprah would one day use these horrifying experiences to unite women in the cause of ending sexual abuse against women and children. Oprah continued to live with her mother, but the care she was receiving was anything but substantial. Shortly after she turned thirteen, Oprah grew unable to deal with her mother's neglect and the constant sexual abuse, so she stole more money from her mother and ran away. The money did not last long and Oprah was soon left looking for a place to stay. With nowhere else to turn, Oprah sought the aid of her pastor, but he too sympathized with Oprah's mother and turned the young girl back over to her mother. Oprah's mother was livid that she would steal money from her, much less run away from home. After a lengthy fight with her mother, Oprah's mother renounced her as her daughter and Oprah was left homeless. Further complicating the matter, Oprah was raped by her uncle and this time became pregnant. Oprah recalls these days as being the darkest days she would encounter in her life. "I hit rock bottom," Oprah recalls. "I became pregnant and hid the pregnancy. I'd intended to kill myself actually. I thought there's no way other than killing myself. I was just planning on how to do it. If

I'd had the internet, I might not be alive because now you can just Google how to do it." As a pregnant, homeless fourteen year old, Oprah was forced to enter a shelter for troubled girls, a situation she describes as "horrifying." Oprah's pregnancy was a difficult one filled with health and emotional struggles. After her baby was born prematurely, he died, leaving Oprah once again without a friend to talk to. Oprah's father however would later view the miscarriage as a "second-chance" for Oprah to enjoy a child's life. Oprah would later concur, saying "I was, in many ways, saved by that and I made a decision that I was going to turn it around." Oprah's mother allowed her to return home for the time being, but the stay was not pleasant. Oprah's mother continually berated her, making her feel inferior and unqualified because of her miscarriage and failed attempt at running away. In later memoirs, Oprah credits these days with making her not want to be a mother. A child placed under such cruel conditions, Oprah's mother made her childhood so unbearable that Oprah was convinced she could never handle the responsibility of having children. Through the constant cruelty, Oprah's mother had effectively silenced her daughter's initial dreams of having a family.

After returning to her mother's home, Oprah enrolled at Lincoln High School in Milwaukee and was given a glimpse of joy when she joined the

Upward Bound Program. This program seeks to give low income children a better chance to attend college after graduation. The program was financed through grants and showed great promise for providing greater education once Oprah graduated. Oprah was so dedicated to the program that her teachers recommended she be transferred from Lincoln High School to the more prestigious Nicolet High School. While the move provided a greater educational experience for Oprah, the wealth of the students was a stark contrast to the poverty from which Oprah emerged. The students were aware of the lower lifestyle lived by Oprah and made sure to remind her of her dismal state. The African-American population of Nicolet High School was not treated well in general. Most of the African-American population actually came from the same homes as the wealthy children where the African-American students were employed as servants. However, the novelty of having an African-American friend far surpassed the racial disagreements. Oprah recalls "In 1968, it was real hip to know a black person, so I was very popular." As Oprah continued in her education at Nicolet High School, she became interested in reading and was soon reading as many books in the library as she could. During an interview with *Good Housekeeping* in 1991, Oprah mentioned that "Books showed me there were possibilities in life…reading gave me hope. For me, it was the open door." During these months, Oprah began giving into peer pressure and would steal more money from her mother in an effort to live the lifestyle of her friends who were not under such a stringent budget. As her mother continued to verbally abuse her, Oprah became less and less transparent with her mother and often lied to her in an effort to go on dates with as many boys as possible. Before long, Oprah's mother became aware of her dishonesty and decided she could no longer control Oprah. Frustrated at Oprah's lack of obedience, Oprah's mother dismissed her from her household and Oprah was sent to live once again with her father. This visit would be different however. Oprah's father actually loved her, and the next few months would give Oprah the academic excellence that would lay the foundation for her future.

 After moving in with her father in Nashville again, Oprah realized her father valued her far more than her mother did. Vernon made sure to keep up with his daughter's education, ensuring she was learning adequately and efficiently. In an effort to help her be the best she could be, Vernon forced Oprah to learn at least five new words a day or she would not be allowed to eat dinner. Additionally, Oprah was required to read one book a week and then write a book report on the book she had just read. While Oprah's life went from neglected to strict, her new life provided structure which would be pivotal in her pursuit of public speaking. In an interview later in life, Oprah credits her father with saving her life. "My father turned my life around by insisting that I be more than I was and by believing that I could be more," recalls a thankful Oprah. "His love of learning showed me the way." Oprah began thriving under the structure of her father and was soon participating in functions at school and at her local church. When just fifteen, Oprah's church chose her to sing with the church choir in a singing engagement in southern California. The experience inspired Oprah and she credits her love of music today with this experience. While in California, the choir toured Beverly Hills and Hollywood, stopping by the Hollywood Walk of Fame. There, Oprah vowed to one day have a star with her name on it. The trip inspired Oprah to become a woman of action and upon her return from the trip, Oprah began leading her peers at school in change. Shortly after her "revival," Oprah took on the role as head of the student council at her school while also being an active member in the school drama club. Under the direction of her drama teachers, Oprah became skilled in the areas of oratory art and disputing. Oprah had truly experienced a life change, a life change that would soon lead to her changing lives.

As Oprah continued to work hard in school while grooming her public speaking abilities, teachers took notice of her work ethic and recommended she participate in an oratory contest sponsored by the Elks Club. Though uninterested at first, Oprah entered the contest and, to the delight of her teachers and father, won the contest. The contest provided Oprah with more than just experience, however; Oprah was awarded a scholarship to Tennessee State University while also grabbing the attention of many prominent public speakers. Shortly after the speaking engagement, Oprah was nominated as an "Outstanding American Teenager" and was invited by President Nixon to the White House to represent the African-American children of Nashville. The trip to the White House led to further change for Oprah. Gone was the face of a victim as Oprah ushered in aspirations of holding influence in Washington D.C. some day. However, Oprah recognized her success would have to have a foundation, a foundation founded on the change she could start in Nashville. Back in Nashville, Oprah had become a recognized face in her school, being voted "Most Popular Girl" her senior year. Later that year, Oprah would enter a speech competition focused on dramatic interpretation, a contest she would not win, but placed second in the nation. As Oprah continued to gain influence in her Nashville, she entered more competitions, with most of them centered on speech and oratory elements. One such contest that was not centered on oration was the Miss Fire Prevention Contest, a beauty pageant of sorts sponsored by the local radio station, WVOL. After Oprah won the competition with ease, station manager John Heidelberg noticed Oprah's charisma and poise and offered the rising star a platform to showcase her talents. John offered Oprah the job of reading newscasts during the afternoon on air. Oprah was elated at the opportunity to gain more practical experience speaking, so she accepted the offer eagerly. The opportunity provided more than simply experience, however: Oprah was paid $100 a week for her work. While Oprah had previously worked as a cashier at a grocery store in Nashville, she was now getting paid to do her favorite thing in life: talk. Oprah's dream to one day "get paid to speak" was finally becoming a reality.

In addition to the Miss Fire Prevention beauty pageant, Oprah entered the Miss Black Tennessee beauty pageant and won it at the age of seventeen. After graduating from East Nashville High School in 1971, Oprah packed up her belongings and headed off to Tennessee State University to study under the financial security of her full scholarship. Tennessee State University, a college with a largely African-American population, offered Oprah the needed security while also offering a qualified higher education. Oprah enrolled as a double major in speech and drama and was on the precipice of the second great milestone in her pursuit of a career with public speaking. While holding accolades as Miss Black Tennessee and Miss Tennessee during her freshman year, Oprah also was offered a job at the CBS affiliated Nashville Columbian Broadcasting System. Desiring to focus on her grades and studies, Oprah turned down the first offer and would turn down a subsequent offer months later. Finally, when the station offered her a job for the third time, Oprah sought the advice and mentoring of one of her speech teachers. After the speech teacher learned of the interest CBS held in her student, she encouraged Oprah to accept the offer, noting that being offered a job by CBS was "the reason people go to college." At only the age of 19, Oprah became a co-anchor of the local evening news shown every night. As she grew into this role, Oprah became the first African-American female to reach the occupation of co-anchor in America, while also being the youngest news anchor nation-wide. Oprah's emergence as the first female African-American to co-anchor a news broadcast was courageous in itself, but further down, there was significantly greater importance than what met the eye. At this time in American's history, race segregation was dominating everything from business transactions to the education system. An African-American in a position of leadership held significant meaning to the African-American community. As just a sophomore in college, Oprah Winfrey was succeeding in changing the world, only through the changes and maturation of her own spirits.

  Oprah became a local sensation around Nashville through her broadcasting efforts at the news station. However, announcing the evening news proved to be away from Oprah's style and natural ability. Oprah knew that her true strength was found in comfort and emotion, two traits that can cause uncomfortable circumstances for viewers if the evening news was not optimistic. Before long, Oprah was struggling to maintain a face of courage when announcing devastation across the world, sometimes even losing her poise when announcing the falling stock prices. The end of her role as co-anchor was inevitable and after nine months of service, Oprah was removed from her position as anchor. She was not fired from the news station however and would continue to serve in lower profile areas of the news station. While this news was anything but encouraging for Oprah, she was still convinced she had found a career she could serve in. For some, Oprah's demotion would have served as an unsurpassable obstacle. However, Oprah recognized she was still in college and was still growing. Following her demotion from WLAC, the CBS affiliate, another news station from Baltimore, WJZ-TV offered Oprah the position of reporter. Oprah considered this a promotion from her current role and accepted the position. Following her acceptance as a reporter, a vacancy in the position of co-anchor allowed Oprah a second chance at once again being the anchor and delivering the nightly news to the homes of the thousands of residencies surrounding Baltimore. Oprah showed greater poise this time and soon deemed herself worthy to move on to a talk show. After moving to co-host *Baltimore is Talking* with Richard Sher, Oprah found the career she had so long been searching for. As host of a talk show, Oprah was free to tackle more controversial topics while also giving the citizens of Baltimore a channel to voice their opinions through. Oprah recounts that she felt so invigorated after every show. "I came off the air and said to myself, 'This is what I should be doing.'" remembers an excited Oprah. "'It's like breathing.'" The audiences loved Oprah and soon, Oprah was seen as the leader of the show with Richard Sher simply acting as another voice of support for Oprah. For the time being, Oprah had found her niche in the media.

Oprah would continue as co-host of *Baltimore is Talking* for the next seven years. While playing host to *Baltimore is Talking*, Oprah also hosted *Dialing for Dollars-Baltimore*. During these seven years, not only were the citizens of Baltimore watching the show; the station manager of the Chicago affiliate for ABC, WLS-TV, had been receiving video cassettes from Oprah's producer, Debra DiMaio, which contained full episodes of Oprah's shows with the intentions that he would hire her. During this time in Oprah's career, the ratings for her talk show were so high that they even trumped Phil Donahue's. Seeing Oprah's influence as being greater than the national icon Phil Donahue was, the manager began greatly considering the possibility of bringing Oprah to Chicago. The ruse worked and WLS-TV offered Oprah a job as anchor of *A.M. Chicago*, a talk show broadcast in the morning in desperate need of a boost in the ratings. Oprah agreed to take over as anchor and moved to Chicago in the crisp chill of January in 1984. As a young but vibrant 29 year old, Oprah was ready to make this television show her next project and hopefully bring it to the standard that *Baltimore is Talking* had achieved. Oprah recalls her first thoughts of Chicago during a trip she had made their the fall before her move."My first day in Chicago, September 4, 1983. I set foot in this city, and just walking down the street, it was like roots, like the motherland. I knew I belonged here," recalls an inspired and encouraged Oprah Winfrey. Oprah's first task on her new show was to shift the focus from women's issues to the latest issues causing controversy and debate in America. As Oprah sought to create a unique television show, Chicago and the world of media watched intently, hoping the newest anchor of *A.M. Chicago* could resurrect the television show.

While Oprah held great optimism and courage for her new show, she also harbored pangs of fear. America was still divided by race, so Oprah was anxious to see how her audience would accept an anchor of color. Also adding to her fear, *A.M. Chicago* was set to air every day at the same time that her major competitor in Baltimore, *The Phil Donahue Show* was also airing. Oprah feared that her initial shows would not be interesting enough and that the audience, and even her colleagues, would switch from her channel and instead watch the show of a national speech icon. Oprah eventually realized that simply fearing the unknown was of no benefit to her show. Oprah rather turned her fear of the unknown into action and worked tirelessly to create a show that would more than rival Phil Donahue's talk show—it would surpass it. As Oprah worked hard each day on her show, her dreams soon became reality and her fears dissipated (along with the popularity of Phil Donahue). After only one month of airing, Oprah's *A.M. Chicago* had equaled the ratings of *The Phil Donahue Show*. Three months after Oprah's takeover of *Chicago A.M.*, her show had surpassed the ratings of *The Phil Donahue Show* and Oprah had won the battle. The program manager for WLS-TV rewarded Oprah for her hard work by renaming *A.M. Chicago* to *The Oprah Winfrey Show* and making the show one hour instead of a half hour. Due to his suffering popularity, Phil Donahue was forced to relocate from blustery Chicago to the safe retreat of New York City. As Oprah developed her new show, the city of Chicago paid respect to the fearless women and most of the city watched her show every morning. In only one year, the viewership of *The Oprah Winfrey Show* skyrocketed to margins of over 150%! Oprah had won the heart of the city by giving her heart to the city.

    Beginning in 1986, *The Oprah Winfrey Show* began being televised nationally and continued to trounce Phil Donahue by holding almost double the viewership that *The Phil Donahue Show* held. Oprah's rise to fame was largely in part to the varied nature of the show. Oprah refused to debate topics for more than one show and was constantly bringing in a barrage of new guests to the show. Oprah is actually credited with being one of the first recorded hosts to host a homosexual couple on a personal television show. Oprah gathered her millions in the audiences through her willingness to hear every opinion in the best interest of equality and co-existing. From the earliest of her shows on her new national program, Oprah demonstrated her ability in being able to interview people from virtually every walk of life. Later, Oprah would back this appreciation with "…we are each responsible for our own life—no other person is or even can be." In the fourth grade, Oprah had told her teacher that she aspired to be a teacher and now, Oprah had been given the platform to teach millions of people at one time. In an article on the rise of Oprah's fame, *TIME Magazine* asserted

> Few people would have bet on Oprah Winfrey's swift rise to host of the most popular talk show on TV. In a field dominated by white males, she is a black female of ample bulk. As interviewers go, she is no match for, say, Phil Donahue… What she lacks in journalistic toughness, she makes up for in plainspoken curiosity, robust humor, and above all, empathy. Guests with sad stories to tell are apt to rouse a tear in Oprah's eye…They in turn often find themselves revealing things they would not imagine telling anyone, much less a national TV audience. It is the talk show as a group therapy session.
>
> For Oprah, her job was hardly work. She enjoyed the national spotlight and proved herself a worthy candidate for such a position.

As *The Oprah Winfrey Show* gained momentum, so did the accolades and reputation. For the first years, the show garnered the reputation as being a tabloid talk show. Despite the usual presence of critics willing to put any aspect of the show into question, many Hollywood celebrities voiced their opinions of support for the growing leader of women across America. Howard Rosenberg from the *Los Angeles Times* noted "She's a roundhouse, a full course meal, big, brassy, loud, aggressive, hyper, laughable, lovable, soulful, tender, low-down, earthy, and hungry. And she knows the way to Phil Donahue's jugular." Martha Bayles from *The Wall Street Journal* echoed this sentiment in a review of *The Oprah Winfrey Show* through which she said these words about Oprah: "It's a relief to see a gab-monger with a fond but realistic assessment of her own cultural and religious roots." Oprah was gaining national attention by simply being herself.

    In 1985, Oprah gathered the spotlight for something other than her role in television. A local movie producer, Quincy Jones, was currently busy with producing a film adaptation of the popular novel *The Color Purple*, written by Alice Walker. In Chicago on business, Quincy Jones was resting in his hotel and watching the local news when he caught the end of one of Oprah's shows. Quincy was currently looking for a woman to play Sofia in the new film and after seeing Oprah, Quincy was convinced she held great potential for playing this role. There was only one problem with his current proposition: Oprah had next to no experience acting and had only been a part of one production following college, *The History of Black Women through Drama and Song*. Apart from the numerous speech classes she had taken during college, Oprah was brand new to the acting field and many thought it rash of Quincy to propose casting her as Sofia. After getting permission from co-producer Steven Spielberg, Quincy cast Oprah and began teaching her the rudiments of acting. After the movie was released, Oprah received an Oscar for her performance while also receiving a Golden Globe for Best Supporting Actress in the film. The highly anticipated film was received very well by the audiences and critics alike. *The Chicago Tribune* gave Oprah's performance particularly high marks and mentioned that the performance was "shockingly good." Oprah was encouraged by the acceptance of the audiences and vowed that she would someday return to the film industry. For now though, it was time to return to her role as permanent host of *The Oprah Winfrey Show*.

While Oprah had intended to return from her performance in *The Color Purple* and work solely for her show, she was further recognized for her performance, which led to other movie producers requesting the talents of Oprah Winfrey. The National Organization for Women reignited the public interest in Oprah by awarding Oprah the "Woman of Achievement Award." In 1986, Oprah was cast as the mother of the main character in *Native Son*, a film adapted from the novel written by Richard Wright. Despite the hard work of Oprah and her fellow cast members, the movie failed to succeed in the box office premiere and the weeks that ensued. Oprah would later admit that having to portray a mother in the film was very hard. She was not a mother and had not had a mother to base her performance on. Despite the film's poor performance, the spotlight it cast on Oprah benefited *The Oprah Winfrey Show* greatly. Oprah continued to push her show forward in the race to be the best television show being broadcasted. Following the film, Oprah would participate in many more films while also providing her voice to add character to a few cartoons. As *The Oprah Winfrey Show* continued to grow, it also began to be recognized with awards for its stellar performance. In 1987, Oprah was recognized as "Best Talk Show Host" and *The Oprah Winfrey Show* received numerous Emmy awards for being the "Best Talk Show." After King World purchased the rights of syndication for *The Oprah Winfrey Show,* the show's success only grew faster. While *The Oprah Winfrey Show* was being broadcast on 138 stations and *The Phil Donahue Show* was being broadcast in 200 stations, *The Oprah Winfrey Show* continued to draw more of an audience than *The Phil Donahue Show* was able to procure. In 1987, Oprah was also able to gain the top ten markets being broadcast in America. For Oprah, her current success was a stark contrast from her early days of being a poor, shoeless girl living in abject poverty, but it was still hardly the climax of her career. Oprah's pinnacle of success still lay before her.

The year 1987 held more importance than just being the year that Oprah launched her namesake show. In 1986, Oprah had met Stedman Graham at a charity event. The billionaire investment mogul caught the eye of Oprah and before the end of the year, the two were dating. During the initial days of their relationship, Stedman would spend weekends at Oprah's condo in Chicago and began hinting at a future that included more than just dating when he left his toothbrush at her condo. After dating for six years, Stedman decided it was time to marry Oprah and proposed to Oprah in their kitchen in 1992. There, in their new home located in Indiana, Stedman Graham asked Oprah to marry him and said "I want you to marry me. I think it's time." Oprah recalls her surprise in his proposal and replied "Ah, that's really great." However, the two would not be wed. After the proposal, the couple decided they were not ready for marriage and decided to postpone the wedding. Later, Oprah stated "What I realized is, I don't want to be married." Later, Oprah would reveal that her life simply was not compatible with that of a married woman's life. Though not married and convinced they never will be, Oprah and Stedman remain faithful to each other and have confessed they do love each other, just not enough to be married. Though repeatedly telling the media that they have no plans to be married, Oprah and Stedman continue to be the focus of rumors stating false marriage dates. Though the seemingly perfect couple will never be married, Oprah says that the relationship demonstrates the ability of women to have a partner while maintaining a full-time career.

    In 1987, Oprah was devoting the majority of her time to her show, but still desired to be involved in dramatic productions. Oprah decided she could best present dramatic productions on controversial topics close to her heart if she owned her own production company. After consulting her manager and receiving positive encouragement from her, Oprah announced the formation of Harpo, Inc. as a film company that would produce films centered on topics that Oprah deemed necessary. Harpo, Inc., Oprah backwards, helped vault *The Oprah Winfrey Show* to the front of the ratings and made Oprah Winfrey the highest paid television talk show host of the day. One series featured by the film production company was *The Women of Brewster Place*, which featured Oprah as a main character along with several other leading women's rights activists of the time. Along with the new success being enjoyed by *The Oprah Winfrey Show*, the show began to take on a new perspective during the early 90s. Shifting from what some had referred to as a tabloid-based feel, Oprah directed her show to tackle more controversial topics like spirituality, meditation, heart disease, and geopolitics. In addition to this new outlook, the show also began focusing on celebrities and showcasing everything from their charity work to their sexual orientation. The show also began to cater to its audience more and planned regular giveaways such as a car for or a trip to Australia for every audience member. Oprah also began gaining access to celebrities that could have been considered highly classified and who rarely granted interviews with the media. In 1993, Oprah netted what has been considered the greatest interview of all time: an interview with the elusive Michael Jackson. After the interview aired, it became fourth on the list of most-watched events and first on the list of most-watched interviews. Following the interview, the success of Oprah's television show began spreading across the borders of America and into the foreign market. In 1993, *The Oprah Winfrey Show* was being broadcast on 99% of the television markets in America while also holding markets in foreign countries such as Saudi Arabia, New Zealand, Japan, and Norway.

In 1992, Oprah had interviewed Marianne Williamson on her show and promoted her book, *A Return to Love*. The interview proved to be the best possible publicity the book could have received and following the show, over 35,000 copies of the book were sold in one day. After just one week following the show, the remaining copies of *A Return to Love,* almost 350,000 copies, had been sold, simply because the book had been promoted on *The Oprah Winfrey*

Show. The success of the book was in stark contrast to the average 10,000 copies sold of most books. Oprah's influence was further demonstrated when over 100,000 copies of *Ageless Body, Timeless Mind* were sold in only one day following the book's promotion on *The Oprah Winfrey Show*. This inspired Oprah and she conceived the plans for an on-air book club. After introducing the club on September 17, 1996, Oprah announced that her goal was "to get the country reading." After releasing a book list for her fans to use when purchasing their books, Oprah instructed her fans to purchase the books and read them ahead of the show next month, in which they would discuss the books they had read. Once again, Oprah's influence made publicity agents for certain books excited and, for one in particular, *The Deep End of the Ocean,* made the publicity agents rich. Following Oprah's announcement to the distributor saying she would be endorsing the book, the distributors knew it would become successful, so they published almost 90,000 more copies than they had originally intended. On the day the show aired, almost 750,000 copies of the book had been printed, and yet this was still not enough to appease the thousands seeking a copy of the book. Following the show, the distributer of *The Deep End of the Ocean* would publish almost 100,000 more copies of the book. The on-air book club cemented Oprah's position as the greatest influence on

America's book industry to date. Television stars, radio hosts, and newspaper columnists combined could not keep up with the rate at which Oprah was sending people to the book stores. However, as Oprah's schedule began to get increasingly busier, she decided to limit the book club and in 2002, decided to discontinue the book club altogether. The book club had provided countless writers with success they arguably would not have had without Oprah's endorsement, and thus once again proved to America that Oprah's influential power was legitimate and perhaps the greatest force of influence in America at the time.

Though Oprah was enjoying the success and popularity her show was giving her, not everyone was as big of a fan of Oprah as her audiences were. In 1998, some of these adversaries of Oprah surfaced when Oprah gave air-time to a story about cattle abuse in Texas. As the headlines read: "Oprah accused of whipping up anti-beef 'lynch mob,'" Oprah was introduced to a group of cattle ranchers from Texas who were less than enthusiastic that Oprah had aired such a demoralizing story. In the show, Oprah had interviewed Howard Lyman who delivered an emotionally charged story on the presence of Mad Cow disease in some of the meat being processed by cattle ranchers. In the interview, Howard revealed that sometimes, cows that are found to have Mad Cow disease are actually fed to other cows in an effort to save the tainted meat by using it. After this revelation was made on air, Oprah replied "It has just stopped me cold from eating another burger!" For anyone else to have said this, it would have been simply a matter of opinion, but for Oprah, the leading influence in America, her simple comment lead to an alarming decrease in demand for meat while subsequently lowering the price of meat across America. This story then received world-wide attention with the British media quoting Howard Lyman in their version of the story, only adding to the crisis being felt by the ranchers across America. The price of meat had already been declining steadily as Americans learned about Mad Cow disease, but Oprah's convictions against eating burgers dramatically increased the decline. The cattle ranchers from Texas opened a class action lawsuit valued at almost $11 million against Oprah. The trial lasted almost five weeks but after those five weeks, a jubilant and vindicated Oprah Winfrey left the court room asserting "Free speech not only lives—it rocks!" One cattleman commented, saying "In today's world of instant and widespread communications, the impact of misinformation can be devastating on the market for perishable agricultural products." Oprah would not be deterred by such a lawsuit and declared "I will continue to use my voice. I believed from the beginning this was an attempt to muzzle that voice in this country and I refuse to be muzzled. I will not change the way I operate!" For Oprah, the protection of her First Amendment rights was important, but more than that, her vindication in this case proved that America was in favor of the influential woman. Oprah was truly feeling the sense of acceptance she had longed for in the days of her childhood.

During the early 2000s, Oprah began to experience more criticism than she had previously felt. Whereas her audience had largely accepted her so willingly since her inception as a talk show host back in Baltimore, some of her critics began to comment on her physical appearance more now that Oprah was firmly seated on good ratings and powerful influence. Oprah never allowed the criticism to shake her and instead let many of her shows center on her struggle with her weight. During one such show, Oprah revealed that her weight gain had come largely due to a romantic relationship that did not develop into the relationship Oprah wanted. Later, Oprah would credit the majority of her weight gain with the lack of approval she was receiving from men. "The reason I gained so much weight in the first place and the reason I had such a sorry history of abusive relationships with men was I just needed approval so much" says Oprah.

> I needed everyone to like me, because I didn't like myself much. So, I'd end up with these cruel, self-absorbed guys who's tell me how selfish I

was, and I'd say 'Oh thank you, you're so right' and be grateful to them because I had no sense that I deserved anything else. This is why I gained so much weight later on. It was the perfect way of cushioning myself against the world's disapproval.

Oprah's own pursuit of gaining approval and love from everyone she met led her to a disappointment that largely resulted in her struggle with weight. Along with a struggle with weight, Oprah later revealed she also struggled deeply with depression during her days in Baltimore. After being involved in an extra-marital affair with a man who was not ready to sever his marriage with his wife, Oprah recalls begging for his love. On her show, Oprah recalls "I wasn't living with him. I'd never lived with anyone—and I thought I was worthless without him. The more he rejected me, the more I wanted him. I felt depleted, powerless. At the end, I was down on the floor on my knees groveling and pleading with him." The rejection led to depression, which ultimately led to Oprah penning a suicide note on September 8, 1981. Oprah addressed the suicide note to her best friend Gayle King in which she implored Gayle to water her plants. Despite all of the drama that ensued, Oprah would later reveal that the suicide note was simply for effect. "That suicide note had been much overplayed," writes Oprah. "I couldn't kill myself. I would be afraid the minute I did it; something really good would happen and I'd miss it." Though Oprah was telling her friends that all was well, Oprah was still searching for love and affection deep down and would not be content until she found such deep love.

Following Oprah's involvement with the married man, she left her relationship with him for another man who offered her love while also not being married. Unfortunately, the man held intense power over Oprah and convinced her to partake in smoking cocaine with him. Oprah would later reveal "I always felt that the drug itself is not the problem but that I was addicted to the man. I can't think of anything I wouldn't have done for that man." However, the promises of happiness and a future disappeared when the man left Oprah, leaving her with more feelings of rejection. Oprah would enter a relationship with another man who used drugs, and this relationship ended worse than the previous one. After Oprah left the man in 1985, the man attempted to sue Oprah for $20 million, claiming she had blocked a book he was writing in which he revealed their drug-related escapades. Though Oprah never even had to testify, the loss of yet another lover left her more broken and hurt, all while being asked to maintain poise on the nightly news broadcasts and talk shows. Oprah would briefly date Reginald Chevalier, in which Oprah described Reginald as being kind and compassionate. This relationship would be a breath of fresh air for a woman who had become so used to rejection and heartbreak. According to Oprah, Reginald actually loved her and the relationship was founded on reciprocity and true love. Oprah would continue dating Reginald until she met Stedman, her current lover, in 1986. For Oprah, the relationships of Reginald and Stedman were, and continue to be, her definition of true love. As a woman who had experienced some of the worst men this world could offer, the true love offered by Reginald and Stedman was the encouragement needed for Oprah to become the influential power she now is.

In 2004, Oprah began working on yet another market she could reach through the announcement of her monthly magazine, *O, the Oprah Magazine*. The magazine was a tremendous success and continues to be one of the most read magazines in America to this day. In 2005, Oprah targeted a new market of influence through the release of her weight loss book, *The Best Life*, co-authored by Bob Greene. Oprah also made news on this book by paying the world's highest advance book fee. Though the fee remains undisclosed, it overtook the former world record held by President Bill Clinton. The book did not perform as well as expected, a surprising element considering the books publicized on Oprah's television show usually succeeded quite nicely. Oprah refused to be discouraged and instead took her talents to yet another market: the radio. On

February 9, 2006, Oprah revealed that she would be starting a new radio station, transmitted by XM Satellite Radio, that would broadcast every hour of every day while hosting previous guests from *The Oprah Winfrey Show* and her personal magazine, *O, the Oprah Magazine*. Oprah began the daily segment *Oprah & Friends* on September 25, 2006 and continues to broadcast this segment from her studio at her Chicago headquarters. Per Oprah's contract, she must broadcast for at least 30 minutes a week for 39 weeks out of the year. Oprah more than doubles this requirement with her daily segment.

During the beginning days of *The Oprah Winfrey Show,* Oprah achieved the status of millionaire after her show became televised nationally by King World Productions. The achievement marked the first of many accomplishments Oprah had vowed to complete having grown up in such abject poverty. After only nine years of being a millionaire, Oprah had accumulated a net worth of almost $350 million, vaulting her way past Bill Cosby on the *Forbes 400* and making her the only African-American woman on the list. Oprah's value has only increased as she has increased her many outlets and by 2000, Oprah was worth $800 million. Such a high net value places Oprah at the forefront of African-American wealth and makes her the richest African-American of the 20th and 21st century. Oprah's wealth has garnered her more than just a comfortable lifestyle; it now serves as a blueprint for others to follow through the economics course *History 298: Oprah Winfrey, the Tycoon*, taught at the University of Illinois. In 2006, Oprah crossed the racial boundaries of her previous awards and became the highest paid television entertainer of America, with a $260 million pay check for her services in 2006. The paycheck more than quadruples that of the second place entertainer, Simon Cowell. Near the end of her show, Oprah was earning almost $275 million a year. In 2003, Oprah achieved billionaire status, and from 2004-2006, *Forbes Magazine* listed Oprah as the sole billionaire in the world who was black. As the culmination of a career centered on hard work and change continued, Oprah overtook the previous CEO of eBay, Meg Whitman, as the most wealthy, self-employed woman in American. While the wealth is an asset to Oprah's life, her true joy lies in having completed what she set out to change. Oprah wanted to change the face of wealth in America, so long dominated by men. Oprah also became even more of a hero to the African-American community with her accolades of wealth. Through the desire and courage to change, Oprah created a lavish lifestyle that will ensure she never relives the tragedy and poverty of her youth.

Rather than simply hoard her wealth, Oprah has become a leading advocate of philanthropy in the world today. In 2004, Oprah had given so much to charities and other aid efforts that she was the first African-American to enter the top 50 in the most generous Americans. Oprah would remain in this segment until 2010. According to Oprah's magazine, Oprah had given almost $400 million just to educational charities by 2012. Oprah was not merely attempting change through the use of her voice; Oprah was leading change through funding. One of Oprah's favorite charitable efforts centers on providing scholarships for under-privileged kids to Morehouse College in Atlanta, Georgia. In 2012, Oprah estimated that she had sent almost 400 children to the college. Oprah has long believed in the effects of ensuring that the staff of one's company or cause be aware of the thankful spirit in which the leader regards his staff. To demonstrate this thankful spirit, Oprah sponsored a trip to Hawaii for the entirety of her 1,065 staff positions along with their families in 2006. Such a kind gesture did not go unnoticed, and Oprah was commended for her actions by *Forbes Magazine*. Oprah was also recognized for her contributions through service to film and television through her television show and occasional humanitarian films. In 2002, Oprah became the first recipient of the Bob Hope Humanitarian Award during the Emmy Awards. While Oprah's voice of leadership has caused great change, Oprah has also made great efforts to ensure that the voice of change has financial stability, making up the difference where needed. In 2013,

Oprah was awarded the Presidential Medal of Freedom by President Obama after she donated $12 million to the Smithsonian National Museum of African-American History and Culture. The award was well deserved and gave notice to a woman who has given hope to those growing up in the same conditions she endured as a child. Due to the philanthropic efforts of Oprah, America has seen schools renovated and lives changed with funding and scholarships.

Oprah was further recognized for her philanthropic efforts when the NAACP awarded her the Spingarn Medal. This medal is given to an African-American whom the NAACP regards as being the most influential African-American of the past year. In 2002, *Christianity Today* went a step further in an article they published titled "The Church of O." In the article, *Christianity Today* documented Oprah as becoming the most influential spiritual leader of the current time period. When asked about her spirituality and apparent new leadership, Oprah replied "I have church with myself: I have church walking down the street. I believe in the God force that lives inside all of us, and once you tap into that, you can do anything." Whereas once raised a Baptist, Oprah was slowly bridging the gaps created by the differences in religion and largely creating a new religion that centered on a humanistic approach. Though an icon of religious freedom in America, Oprah received much criticism for a show following the September 11 attacks in which she noted that Islam is "the most misunderstood of the three major religions" and calling it a religion of peace. Oprah would later recant such political views while maintaining that Islam was not to blame for the attacks. Oprah has also played a major role in the political field, arguably being the driving force behind President Obama's election in 2008. After Oprah began traveling with the then-presidential candidate, President Obama's standing in the polls dramatically increased. In an episode of *The Oprah Winfrey Show*, Oprah gave the sole endorsement of her show, an endorsement of President Obama for president in 2008. Following the elections, an independent study from the University of Maryland found that Oprah had contributed over one million votes to the campaign of President Obama simply through the influence of her endorsement. Oprah would later come under fire for being what Ben Shapiro called "extremely biased in her choices of candidates being featured on her show." Oprah denied the allegations saying that President Obama had only come on her show before he had declared his intentions to run. Following the accusations, Oprah would not endorse nor have another candidate on her television show. Still, no one can discount the profound influence Oprah had on the politics in America. The influence was so great that Rod Blagojevich, the governor of Illinois, reportedly offered Oprah the vacant senate seat held by

President Obama. Oprah declined the offer stating she was not interested in being a senator. Oprah's interest in politics seemingly died down for the years following, until the election of President Donald Trump in 2016. Following his election, Stedman Graham reported that Oprah was interested in running for president in 2020. Such a report came on the heels of Kanye West also announcing his interest in running. In an interview with *The Los Angeles Times*, Stedman reported that Oprah's running "would be up to the people. She would absolutely do it if they wanted." President Donald Trump has long maintained that he would "beat Oprah if she even thought of running." While potential candidates for president surface for president long before the race begins, political analysts have long held that Oprah's influence could be the difference in an election between her and a Republican candidate. "With influence like Oprah's," asserts Jeff Thompson of *The Guardian*, "Oprah could feasibly win the campaign through simply campaigning through her various personal mediums of influence."

    All good things come to an end. Such truth leaves people both sad that the good can no longer continue while also leaving the people happy for the good memories imparted upon them by the good times. On May 25, 2011, Oprah held the last episode of *The Oprah Winfrey Show*. During the show, some audience members had to be lead out simply because they were unable to cope with the loss of a daily television show featuring Oprah. Oprah announced she had purchased *Discovery Health Channel* through Discovery Communications and would be changing the cable channel to *OWN: Oprah Winfrey Network*. The change shocked fans but gave them anticipation as to what the new channel would hold. During the series finale, Oprah was the sole host, dismissing the usual format in which she hosted a guest. At the end of the episode, Oprah invited the entirety of her staff to the stage to wish them gratitude for their support and hard work over the years. Along with her sentiments of thankfulness, Oprah aired the fan-voted best moments from *The Oprah Winfrey Show*. Celebrating the end of a successful television show, Oprah remarked "I won't say 'goodbye.' 'I'll just say until we meet again'" and left the stage, giving high-fives to members of the audience as she made her way out of the studio for one last time. OWN had launched five months earlier, but still left a void in which fans wanted their daily dose of the "Oprah affect." After seeing the initial broadcasts were able to procure an audience of over 80 million viewers, Oprah decided she would begin the second television series of her career, *Oprah Prime*. *Oprah Prime*, a prime-time talk show, would once again focus on the issues Oprah had so long discussed on her television series, while granting her the liberty of being her own boss in this new setting. Under the success of OWN, Oprah was able to launch her new television show and reach the audiences she had so long enjoyed interacting with. The ratings from *The Oprah Winfrey Show* carried over and *Oprah Prime* maintains the highest ratings of any day-time television show in America. Following the announcement of her new television show, Oprah was also added to the list of special contributors of *60 Minutes* on CBS. For Oprah, the transition from simply her own television show to her own television network was filled with uncertainty, the principles of faith and courage gave birth to her next step in life, *Oprah Prime*. Through embracing the uncertain, Oprah was able to live her best life while gaining unexpected blessings along the way.

    During a commencement address in 2015 at Smith College, Oprah re-told the story of her rise to fame in front of the thousands of students and parents attending the graduation ceremony. During the commencement address, Oprah revealed the secret to her success as being "the power of service." Oprah revealed that her most successful shows came from the shows that paralleled her true convictions and that showcased her morals. In the speech, Oprah compelled the audience to do what they loved through six simple steps that included believing that what one is doing is vitally important while also taking time to prioritize self-awareness. The speech was largely regarded has her greatest address and truly gave the audience the key to living the life Oprah has so long lived. Through the life of Oprah Winfrey, relatively every audience of people can be encouraged. From those living in impoverished conditions to those at the top of the world in regards to financial stability, Oprah's story applies to and can be lived out by everyone. Perhaps Oprah's greatest conviction in life comes through her quote "You don't become what you want, you become what you believe." For Oprah, her wants had so long centered on acceptance and true love, but until she actually loved and accepted others, she found her pursuit in vain. Oprah has revealed that her powerful influence has tempted her at times to use such power for personal gain, but through refusing to give in to such temptations, Oprah has not only changed the lives of millions, she has changed her own life. In an interview with *Good Housekeeping,* Oprah said "Do the one thing you think you cannot do. Fail at it. Try again. Do better the second time. The only people who never tumble are those who never mount the high wire." Oprah failed more times than she remembers, but through improving before her second chance, Oprah became the wealthy, influential person she now is. The life of Oprah Winfrey has and will continue to encourage every heart on earth that true success is found through true service to mankind.

Printed by Amazon Italia Logistica S.r.l.
Torrazza Piemonte (TO), Italy